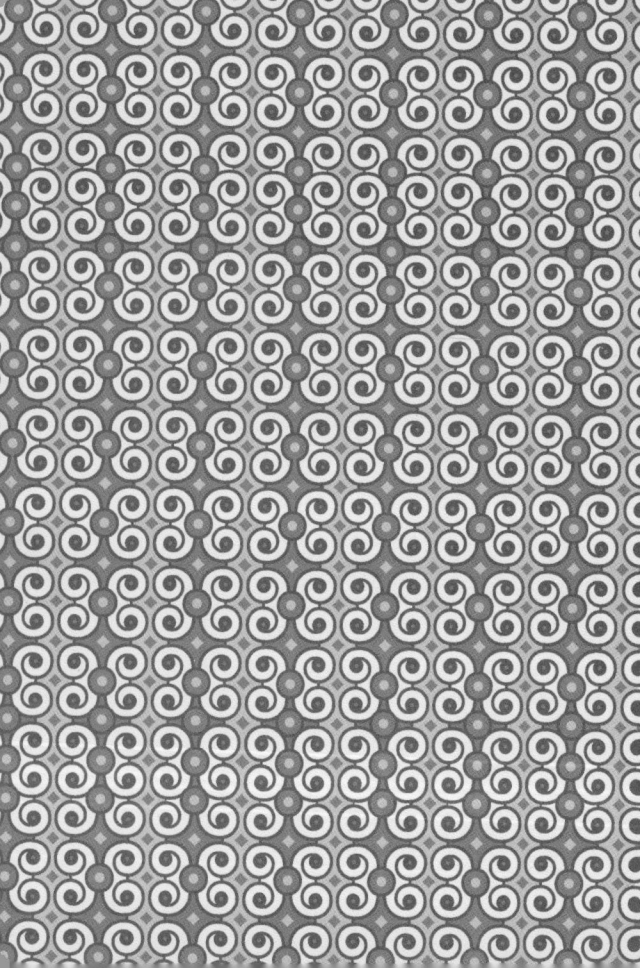

Wine is the most civilized thing
in the world.

—ERNEST HEMINGWAY

Recorded by

checklist for a wine tasting

* 1 corkscrew
* 1 glass per person for each wine
* 1 sheet of paper marked with the wine letters
* 2 plastic cups per person—one for water, one to act as the spittoon
* Paper and pencils
* Large carafe of water or sparkling mineral water
* Water biscuits or bread (optional)
* Tissues or paper napkins
* Receptacle for collecting waste wine

wine tasting order

Since heavier and sweeter wines can overpower lighter wines and influence the taster's experience, wines should be tasted in the following order:

* Sparkling wines
* Light whites
* Heavy whites
* Roses
* Light reds
* Heavy reds
* Sweet wines

eight steps to tasting wine

1. Check the glass for any unpleasant smells.

2. Pour a small amount of wine into the glass.

3. Check the appearance and color of the wine.

4. Swirl the wine in the glass.

5. Take a deep sniff of the wine and write a descriptive note.

6. Take a mouthful of wine and roll it around in your mouth.

7. Spit out the wine and write a descriptive note.

8. Consider the finish of the wine and complete your notes.

how to taste wine

To taste wine all you need are your own senses of sight, smell, and taste—plus a little practice. After all, you can easily tell the difference between pineapples and strawberries. It is simply a matter of adding to the taste memory you already have by making a conscious effort to notice the different aromas and flavors of each wine as you taste it.

appearance and color

Check that the glass is clean by giving it a good sniff before pouring the wine. It should smell of nothing at all. Pour the wine into the glass so that it is a quarter full. Hold the glass against a white background and look at the wine. What you see can tell you something about the age of the wine and where it might have come from. It may also indicate a fault in the wine.

nose

The second step is to smell the wine. The bouquet or aroma that comes off the wine is known to professional tasters as the "nose." The best way to assess the nose is to hold the glass firmly by the stem and swirl the wine in the bowl. The swirling action is important as it adds a little oxygen to the wine and helps to release all the aromas. Place your nose close to the glass and take a good sniff. What do these aromas remind you of? These comparisons are the building blocks for your own taste memory.

palate

The third step is to taste the wine to see if your palate confirms the analysis you have made on the nose. Is the wine as fresh and fruity as you thought it was on the nose, or is it rather disappointing? To experience all the attributes of a wine you must make sure that the wine is rolled all around the mouth and over the entire surface of the tongue. This enables the bitterness taste buds to come into play. After you've experienced the full sensation the wine can be spit out. Then note your finishing comments.

conclusions

Using your notes on the color, nose, and palate of the wine, make an overall assessment of the wine. This is your chance to sum up the wine in a way that will be useful to you in the future. To do this you can follow key words, keeping it simple. Don't wait to think about your notes for too long—your all-important first impressions will have disappeared. You'll want to be distinct so when you look back you'll remember exactly what you experienced.

white grape varieties

* Chardonnay: butter, honey, apple, pineapple, mango, tropical fruits
* Gewürztraminer: lychee, spice, pepper, flowers, roses
* Muscadet: apple, honey, stone
* Muscat: grape, orange rind
* Riesling: citrus fruit, grapefruit, flowers, oil, gasoline
* Sauvignon Blanc: gooseberry, fresh leaves, mint, grass, asparagus
* Sémillon: lemon, melon, pineapple, tropical fruits, peach, nuts, oil, lanolin
* Trebbiano/Ugni Blanc: almond, honey, minerals

WINE/VARIETY: ·

DATE TASTED: ·

REGION: ·

VINTAGE: ·

APPEARANCE AND COLOR: ·

NOSE: ·

PALATE: ·

CONCLUSION: ·

white wine

WINE/VARIETY:

DATE TASTED:

REGION:

VINTAGE:

APPEARANCE AND COLOR:

NOSE:

PALATE:

CONCLUSION:

white wine

WINE/VARIETY:

DATE TASTED:

REGION:

VINTAGE:

APPEARANCE AND COLOR:

NOSE:

PALATE:

CONCLUSION:

white wine

WINE/VARIETY:

DATE TASTED:

REGION:

VINTAGE:

APPEARANCE AND COLOR:

NOSE:

PALATE:

CONCLUSION:

WINE/VARIETY: ·

DATE TASTED: ·

REGION: ·

VINTAGE: ·

APPEARANCE AND COLOR: ·

NOSE: ·

PALATE: ·

CONCLUSION: ·

white wine

WINE/VARIETY:

DATE TASTED:

REGION:

VINTAGE:

APPEARANCE AND COLOR:

NOSE:

PALATE:

CONCLUSION:

What is the definition of good wine?
It should start and end with a smile.

—WILLIAM SOKOLIN

··· WINE/VARIETY: ·····································

··· DATE TASTED: ·····································

··· REGION: ·····································

··· VINTAGE: ·····································

··· APPEARANCE AND COLOR: ·····················

··· NOSE: ·····································

··· PALATE: ·····································

··· CONCLUSION: ·····································

white wine

WINE/VARIETY:

DATE TASTED:

REGION:

VINTAGE:

APPEARANCE AND COLOR:

NOSE:

PALATE:

CONCLUSION:

white wine

··· WINE/VARIETY: ·······································

··· DATE TASTED: ··

··· REGION: ··

··· VINTAGE: ···

··· APPEARANCE AND COLOR: ·······························

··· NOSE: ··

··· PALATE: ··

··· CONCLUSION: ··

WINE/VARIETY:

DATE TASTED:

REGION:

VINTAGE:

APPEARANCE AND COLOR:

NOSE:

PALATE:

CONCLUSION:

WINE/VARIETY:

DATE TASTED:

REGION:

VINTAGE:

APPEARANCE AND COLOR:

NOSE:

PALATE:

CONCLUSION:

——————————————————————————————— white wine —

····· WINE/VARIETY: ···

···· DATE TASTED: ··

···· REGION: ···

···· VINTAGE: ··

····APPEARANCE AND COLOR: ··

···· NOSE: ···

····PALATE: ··

···· CONCLUSION: ···

————————————————————————— white wine —

·· WINE/VARIETY: ·······································

·· DATE TASTED: ··

·· REGION: ···

·· VINTAGE: ··

·· APPEARANCE AND COLOR: ·······························

·· NOSE: ···

·· PALATE: ···

·· CONCLUSION: ···

··· WINE/VARIETY: ···

··· DATE TASTED: ···

··· REGION: ···

··· VINTAGE: ··

··· APPEARANCE AND COLOR: ·····························

·· NOSE: ···

··· PALATE: ···

··· CONCLUSION: ···

··· tasting suggestions ···················

If you like the idea of serving white wine with
cheese, here are some combinations you might
like to try:

* Soft creamy cheese with German Riesling
  Kabinett

* Goat's cheese with Sancerre, Sauvignon de
  Touraine, or California Fumé Blanc

* Semi-hard cheese with Australian Rhine
  Riesling

* Soft creamy cheese with Champagne or
  California sparkling wine

* Mature cheddar with Sauvignon Blanc from
  New Zealand

* Smoked cheese with a very oaky
  Chardonnay

···· WINE/VARIETY: ······································

···· DATE TASTED: ······································

···· REGION: ······································

···· VINTAGE: ······································

···· APPEARANCE AND COLOR: ······································

···· NOSE: ······································

···· PALATE: ······································

···· CONCLUSION: ······································

·· WINE/VARIETY: ···

·· DATE TASTED: ··

·· REGION: ···

·· VINTAGE: ··

·· APPEARANCE AND COLOR: ···································

·· NOSE: ···

·· PALATE: ···

·· CONCLUSION: ···

white wine

WINE/VARIETY:

DATE TASTED:

REGION:

VINTAGE:

APPEARANCE AND COLOR:

NOSE:

PALATE:

CONCLUSION:

————————————————————— white wine —

· · · WINE/VARIETY: ·

· · · DATE TASTED: ·

· · · REGION: ·

· · · VINTAGE: ·

· · · APPEARANCE AND COLOR: ·

· · · NOSE: ·

· · · PALATE: ·

· · · CONCLUSION: ·

white wine

WINE/VARIETY: ·

DATE TASTED: ·

REGION: ·

VINTAGE: ·

APPEARANCE AND COLOR: ·

NOSE: ·

PALATE: ·

CONCLUSION: ·

———————————————————————— white wine —

· · · WINE/VARIETY: ·

· · · DATE TASTED: ·

· · · REGION: ·

· · · VINTAGE: ·

· · · APPEARANCE AND COLOR: ·

· · · NOSE: ·

· · · PALATE: ·

· · · CONCLUSION: ·

Wine is constant proof that God loves us
and loves to see us happy.

—BENJAMIN FRANKLIN

WINE/VARIETY:

DATE TASTED:

REGION:

VINTAGE:

APPEARANCE AND COLOR:

NOSE:

PALATE:

CONCLUSION:

white wine

WINE/VARIETY: ·

DATE TASTED: ·

REGION: ·

VINTAGE: ·

APPEARANCE AND COLOR: ·

NOSE: ·

PALATE: ·

CONCLUSION: ·

white wine

... WINE/VARIETY: ...

... DATE TASTED: ...

... REGION: ...

... VINTAGE: ...

... APPEARANCE AND COLOR: ...

... NOSE: ...

... PALATE: ...

... CONCLUSION: ...

white wine

··· WINE/VARIETY: ··

··· DATE TASTED: ···

··· REGION: ···

··· VINTAGE: ··

··· APPEARANCE AND COLOR: ···

··· NOSE: ···

··· PALATE: ···

··· CONCLUSION: ···

··· WINE/VARIETY: ··

··· DATE TASTED: ···

··· REGION: ··

··· VINTAGE: ···

··· APPEARANCE AND COLOR: ··································

··· NOSE: ··

··· PALATE: ··

··· CONCLUSION: ··

··· WINE/VARIETY: ···

··· DATE TASTED: ···

··· REGION: ···

··· VINTAGE: ··

··· APPEARANCE AND COLOR: ···

··· NOSE: ···

··· PALATE: ···

··· CONCLUSION: ··

—— white wine ——

WINE/VARIETY: ....

DATE TASTED: ....

REGION: ....

VINTAGE: ....

APPEARANCE AND COLOR: ....

NOSE: ....

PALATE: ....

CONCLUSION: ....

··· WINE/VARIETY: ··

··· DATE TASTED: ···

··· REGION: ··

··· VINTAGE: ···

··· APPEARANCE AND COLOR: ·······························

··· NOSE: ··

··· PALATE: ··

··· CONCLUSION: ··

best cellar *

List your favorite stores to buy wine, and if they offer wine tastings, write down the times and days they occur.

————————————————————————————— white wine —

··· WINE/VARIETY: ···································

·· DATE TASTED: ····································

·· REGION: ···

·· VINTAGE: ··

·· APPEARANCE AND COLOR: ····························

·· NOSE: ··

·· PALATE: ···

·· CONCLUSION: ·····································

white wine

WINE/VARIETY:

DATE TASTED:

REGION:

VINTAGE:

APPEARANCE AND COLOR:

NOSE:

PALATE:

CONCLUSION:

WINE/VARIETY:

DATE TASTED:

REGION:

VINTAGE:

APPEARANCE AND COLOR:

NOSE:

PALATE:

CONCLUSION:

white wine

WINE/VARIETY:

DATE TASTED:

REGION:

VINTAGE:

APPEARANCE AND COLOR:

NOSE:

PALATE:

CONCLUSION:

white wine

WINE/VARIETY:

DATE TASTED:

REGION:

VINTAGE:

APPEARANCE AND COLOR:

NOSE:

PALATE:

CONCLUSION:

white wine

WINE/VARIETY:

DATE TASTED:

REGION:

VINTAGE:

APPEARANCE AND COLOR:

NOSE:

PALATE:

CONCLUSION:

white wine

WINE/VARIETY:

DATE TASTED:

REGION:

VINTAGE:

APPEARANCE AND COLOR:

NOSE:

PALATE:

CONCLUSION:

Wine gives courage and makes men
more apt for passion.

—OVID

—————————————————————————————— white wine ——

··· WINE/VARIETY: ··

··· DATE TASTED: ··

··· REGION: ··

··· VINTAGE: ··

··· APPEARANCE AND COLOR: ····································

··· NOSE: ···

··· PALATE: ···

··· CONCLUSION: ···

white wine

WINE/VARIETY:

DATE TASTED:

REGION:

VINTAGE:

APPEARANCE AND COLOR:

NOSE:

PALATE:

CONCLUSION:

white wine

WINE/VARIETY:

DATE TASTED:

REGION:

VINTAGE:

APPEARANCE AND COLOR:

NOSE:

PALATE:

CONCLUSION:

— white wine —

WINE/VARIETY:

DATE TASTED:

REGION:

VINTAGE:

APPEARANCE AND COLOR:

NOSE:

PALATE:

CONCLUSION:

· · WINE/VARIETY: ·

· · DATE TASTED: ·

· · REGION: ·

· · VINTAGE: ·

· · APPEARANCE AND COLOR: ·

· · NOSE: ·

· · PALATE: ·

· · CONCLUSION: ·

white wine

· · · WINE/VARIETY: ·

· · · DATE TASTED: ·

· · · REGION: ·

· · · VINTAGE: ·

· · · APPEARANCE AND COLOR: ·

· · · NOSE: ·

· · · PALATE: ·

· · · CONCLUSION: ·

· · WINE/VARIETY: ·

· · DATE TASTED: ·

· · REGION: ·

· · VINTAGE: ·

· · APPEARANCE AND COLOR: ·

· · NOSE: ·

· · PALATE: ·

· · CONCLUSION: ·

white wine

WINE/VARIETY:

DATE TASTED:

REGION:

VINTAGE:

APPEARANCE AND COLOR:

NOSE:

PALATE:

CONCLUSION:

red grape varieties

* Cabernet Franc: black currant, grass, fresh leaves

* Cabernet Sauvignon: black currant, cedar, mint

* Gamay: cherry, raspberry, strawberry

* Grenache/Garnacha: blackberry, plum

* Merlot: black currant, plum, mint, raisins

* Nebbiolo: prune, raisins, tobacco, tar

* Pinot Noir: strawberry, plum, cooked beet, chocolate, farmyards, cheese, licorice

* Sangiovese: cherry, herbs, tobacco

* Syrah/Shiraz: raspberry, plum, black currant, chocolate, coffee, leather, tar, pepper

* Zinfandel: blackberry, berry fruits

————————————————————————— red wine —

··· WINE/VARIETY: ··

··· DATE TASTED: ···

··· REGION: ··

··· VINTAGE: ···

··· APPEARANCE AND COLOR: ··

··· NOSE: ··

··· PALATE: ··

··· CONCLUSION: ··

WINE/VARIETY:

DATE TASTED:

REGION:

VINTAGE:

APPEARANCE AND COLOR:

NOSE:

PALATE:

CONCLUSION:

────────────────────────── red wine ─

··· WINE/VARIETY: ···

··· DATE TASTED: ··

··· REGION: ···

··· VINTAGE: ··

··· APPEARANCE AND COLOR: ···

··· NOSE: ···

··· PALATE: ···

··· CONCLUSION: ···

red wine

WINE/VARIETY:

DATE TASTED:

REGION:

VINTAGE:

APPEARANCE AND COLOR:

NOSE:

PALATE:

CONCLUSION:

————————————————— red wine —

WINE/VARIETY:

DATE TASTED:

REGION:

VINTAGE:

APPEARANCE AND COLOR:

NOSE:

PALATE:

CONCLUSION:

────────────────────────────── red wine ──

··· WINE/VARIETY: ·······································

··· DATE TASTED: ··

··· REGION: ··

··· VINTAGE: ···

··· APPEARANCE AND COLOR: ·······························

··· NOSE: ··

··· PALATE: ··

··· CONCLUSION: ···

————————————————————————— red wine —

· · WINE/VARIETY: ·

· · · DATE TASTED: ·

· · · REGION: ·

· · · VINTAGE: ·

· · APPEARANCE AND COLOR: ·

· · · NOSE: ·

· · · PALATE: ·

· · · CONCLUSION: ·

WINE/VARIETY:

DATE TASTED:

REGION:

VINTAGE:

APPEARANCE AND COLOR:

NOSE:

PALATE:

CONCLUSION:

I cook with wine, sometimes I even
add it to the food.

—W.C. FIELDS

WINE/VARIETY:

DATE TASTED:

REGION:

VINTAGE:

APPEARANCE AND COLOR:

NOSE:

PALATE:

CONCLUSION:

red wine

WINE/VARIETY:

DATE TASTED:

REGION:

VINTAGE:

APPEARANCE AND COLOR:

NOSE:

PALATE:

CONCLUSION:

—— red wine —

WINE/VARIETY:

DATE TASTED:

REGION:

VINTAGE:

APPEARANCE AND COLOR:

NOSE:

PALATE:

CONCLUSION:

WINE/VARIETY:

DATE TASTED:

REGION:

VINTAGE:

APPEARANCE AND COLOR:

NOSE:

PALATE:

CONCLUSION:

red wine

- - - WINE/VARIETY: -

- - - DATE TASTED: -

- - - REGION: -

- - - VINTAGE: -

- - - APPEARANCE AND COLOR: -

- - - NOSE: -

- - - PALATE: -

- - - CONCLUSION: -

···· WINE/VARIETY: ···

···· DATE TASTED: ···

···· REGION: ···

···· VINTAGE: ···

···· APPEARANCE AND COLOR: ·······························

···· NOSE: ···

···· PALATE: ···

···· CONCLUSION: ···

light or heavy?

Here is a guide to the kind of body that you can expect from some popular reds.

Lighter Wines
* Australian Shiraz blends (new style)
* Bardolino from Italy
* Beaujolais from France
* Bulgarian country wines
* Burgundy from France
* French Vin de Pays
* Merlot from European countries
* Simple blended red wine from California
* Valpolicella from Italy

Medium Wines
* Some Australian Shiraz/Cabernet blends
* Bordeaux from France
* Bergerac from France
* Bulgarian Cabernet Sauvignon
* Chianti from Italy

* Corbières from France
* Côtes du Rhône from France
* Languedoc-Roussillon wines from France
* Merlot from California, Australia, and Chile
* Minervois from France
* Pinot Noir from California, Australia, and Chile

Heavy Wines
* Australian Shiraz (old style)
* Barolo from Italy
* Cabernet Sauvignon from Australia, California, Chile, and New Zealand
* Cahors from France
* Châteauneuf-du-Pape from France
* Dão from Portugal
* Fitou from France
* Penedès wines from Spain
* Portuguese red wines
* Rioja from Spain

—————————————————————————————————— red wine ——

··· WINE/VARIETY: ···

··· DATE TASTED: ··

··· REGION: ···

··· VINTAGE: ··

··· APPEARANCE AND COLOR: ···

··· NOSE: ···

··· PALATE: ··

··· CONCLUSION: ··

red wine

WINE/VARIETY: ·

DATE TASTED: ·

REGION: ·

VINTAGE: ·

APPEARANCE AND COLOR: ·

NOSE: ·

PALATE: ·

CONCLUSION: ·

··· WINE/VARIETY: ···································

··· DATE TASTED: ···································

··· REGION: ···································

··· VINTAGE: ···································

··· APPEARANCE AND COLOR: ···················

··· NOSE: ···································

··· PALATE: ···································

··· CONCLUSION: ···································

red wine

WINE/VARIETY:

DATE TASTED:

REGION:

VINTAGE:

APPEARANCE AND COLOR:

NOSE:

PALATE:

CONCLUSION:

—————————————————————— red wine —

· · · WINE/VARIETY: ·

· · · DATE TASTED: ·

· · · REGION: ·

· · · VINTAGE: ·

· · · APPEARANCE AND COLOR: ·

· · · NOSE: ·

· · · PALATE: ·

· · · CONCLUSION: ·

WINE/VARIETY:

DATE TASTED:

REGION:

VINTAGE:

APPEARANCE AND COLOR:

NOSE:

PALATE:

CONCLUSION:

··· WINE/VARIETY: ·······················

··· DATE TASTED: ·······················

··· REGION: ·······························

··· VINTAGE: ·····························

··· APPEARANCE AND COLOR: ···············

··· NOSE: ·································

··· PALATE: ·······························

··· CONCLUSION: ··························

Come, come, good wine is a good
familiar creature if it be well used;
exclaim no more against it.

—WILLIAM SHAKESPEARE

—————————————————————————— red wine ——

WINE/VARIETY:

DATE TASTED:

REGION:

VINTAGE:

APPEARANCE AND COLOR:

NOSE:

PALATE:

CONCLUSION:

WINE/VARIETY:

DATE TASTED:

REGION:

VINTAGE:

APPEARANCE AND COLOR:

NOSE:

PALATE:

CONCLUSION:

—————————————————————————————————— red wine ——

·· WINE/VARIETY: ···

·· DATE TASTED: ···

·· REGION: ···

·· VINTAGE: ··

·· APPEARANCE AND COLOR: ··

·· NOSE: ···

·· PALATE: ···

·· CONCLUSION: ···

————————————— red wine —

··· WINE/VARIETY: ·······································

··· DATE TASTED: ···

··· REGION: ···

··· VINTAGE: ··

··· APPEARANCE AND COLOR: ·······························

··· NOSE: ···

··· PALATE: ···

··· CONCLUSION: ···

WINE/VARIETY:

DATE TASTED:

REGION:

VINTAGE:

APPEARANCE AND COLOR:

NOSE:

PALATE:

CONCLUSION:

WINE/VARIETY:

DATE TASTED:

REGION:

VINTAGE:

APPEARANCE AND COLOR:

NOSE:

PALATE:

CONCLUSION:

top of the vine *

Write down wines you've read about in an
article or received a positive recommendation
about from a friend that you want to taste.

WINE/VARIETY:

DATE TASTED:

REGION:

VINTAGE:

APPEARANCE AND COLOR:

NOSE:

PALATE:

CONCLUSION:

————————————————— red wine —————

WINE/VARIETY:

DATE TASTED:

REGION:

VINTAGE:

APPEARANCE AND COLOR:

NOSE:

PALATE:

CONCLUSION:

—————————————————————————————— red wine —

WINE/VARIETY:

DATE TASTED:

REGION:

VINTAGE:

APPEARANCE AND COLOR:

NOSE:

PALATE:

CONCLUSION:

_____ red wine _____

WINE/VARIETY: ....

DATE TASTED: ....

REGION: ....

VINTAGE: ....

APPEARANCE AND COLOR: ....

NOSE: ....

PALATE: ....

CONCLUSION: ....

————————————————————————————— red wine —

· · · WINE/VARIETY: ·

· · · DATE TASTED: ·

· · · REGION: ·

· · · VINTAGE: ·

· · · APPEARANCE AND COLOR: ·

· · · NOSE: ·

· · · PALATE: ·

· · · CONCLUSION: ·

··· WINE/VARIETY: ··

··· DATE TASTED: ··

··· REGION: ··

··· VINTAGE: ··

··· APPEARANCE AND COLOR: ·····························

··· NOSE: ··

··· PALATE: ··

···· CONCLUSION: ··

— red wine —

··· WINE/VARIETY: ·····································

··· DATE TASTED: ·······································

··· REGION: ···

··· VINTAGE: ··

··· APPEARANCE AND COLOR: ·····························

··· NOSE: ···

··· PALATE: ···

··· CONCLUSION: ··

Wine cheers the sad,
revives the old, inspires the young,
makes weariness forget his toil.

—LORD BYRON

——— red wine ———

WINE/VARIETY:

DATE TASTED:

REGION:

VINTAGE:

APPEARANCE AND COLOR:

NOSE:

PALATE:

CONCLUSION:

red wine

WINE/VARIETY:

DATE TASTED:

REGION:

VINTAGE:

APPEARANCE AND COLOR:

NOSE:

PALATE:

CONCLUSION:

red wine

WINE/VARIETY:

DATE TASTED:

REGION:

VINTAGE:

APPEARANCE AND COLOR:

NOSE:

PALATE:

CONCLUSION:

··· WINE/VARIETY: ···

··· DATE TASTED: ··

··· REGION: ···

··· VINTAGE: ··

··· APPEARANCE AND COLOR: ···

··· NOSE: ···

··· PALATE: ···

··· CONCLUSION: ···

red wine

WINE/VARIETY: ....

DATE TASTED: ....

REGION: ....

VINTAGE: ....

APPEARANCE AND COLOR: ....

NOSE: ....

PALATE: ....

CONCLUSION: ....

WINE/VARIETY:

DATE TASTED:

REGION:

VINTAGE:

APPEARANCE AND COLOR:

NOSE:

PALATE:

CONCLUSION:

red wine

WINE/VARIETY: ....

DATE TASTED: ....

REGION: ....

VINTAGE: ....

APPEARANCE AND COLOR: ....

NOSE: ....

PALATE: ....

CONCLUSION: ....

WINE/VARIETY:

DATE TASTED:

REGION:

VINTAGE:

APPEARANCE AND COLOR:

NOSE:

PALATE:

CONCLUSION:

··· You can use these pages to record notes ·········
── about sweet wines, rosés, sparkling wines, ───
··· or other wines that don't fit into a white or ·····
── red category. Before you drink it, however, ───
··· think about how light or heavy and how dry ····
── or sweet the wine is to determine if it ─────
··· should come near the beginning or the end ······
── of the tasting. ────────────────

———————————————————————— assorted wine —

··· WINE/VARIETY: ··

··· DATE TASTED: ···

··· REGION: ···

··· VINTAGE: ··

··· APPEARANCE AND COLOR: ·······························

··· NOSE: ···

··· PALATE: ···

··· CONCLUSION: ··

··· WINE/VARIETY: ·······································

··· DATE TASTED: ·······································

··· REGION: ···

··· VINTAGE: ··

··· APPEARANCE AND COLOR: ·······························

··· NOSE: ···

··· PALATE: ···

··· CONCLUSION: ···

··· WINE/VARIETY: ··

··· DATE TASTED: ···

··· REGION: ··

··· VINTAGE: ···

··· APPEARANCE AND COLOR: ··

··· NOSE: ··

··· PALATE: ··

··· CONCLUSION: ··

sommelier central *

When you're not hosting tastings in your
own home, which restaurants or wine bars
do you visit for a taste of their wine list?

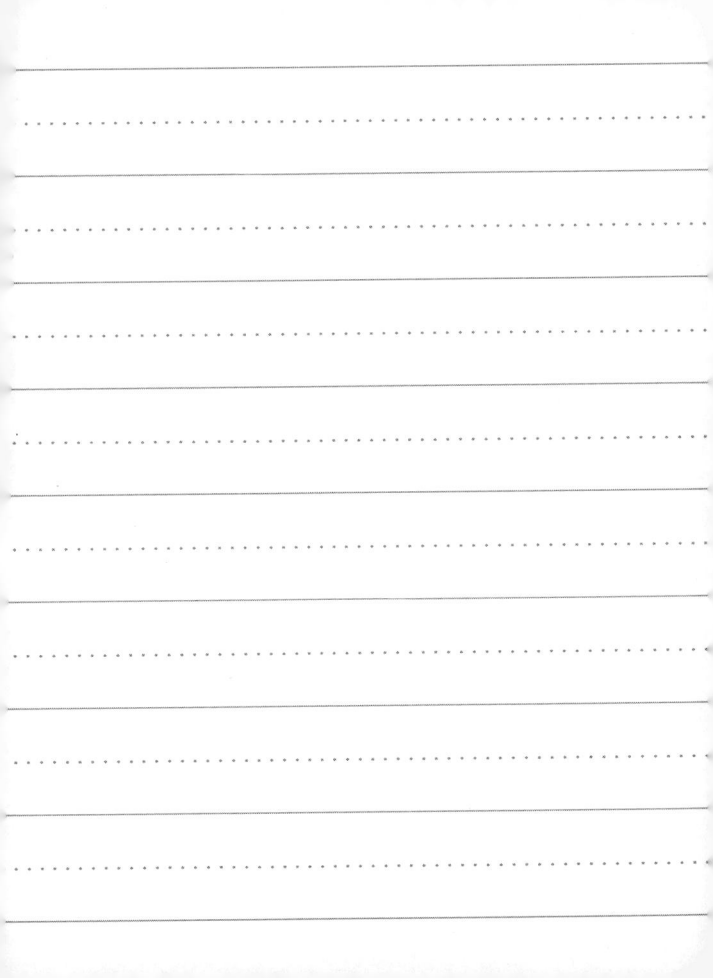

··· WINE/VARIETY: ·······································

··· DATE TASTED: ·······································

··· REGION: ···

··· VINTAGE: ··

··· APPEARANCE AND COLOR: ·······························

··· NOSE: ···

··· PALATE: ···

··· CONCLUSION: ···

· · · WINE/VARIETY: ·

· · · DATE TASTED: ·

· · · REGION: ·

· · · VINTAGE: ·

· · · APPEARANCE AND COLOR: ·

· · · NOSE: ·

· · · PALATE: ·

· · · CONCLUSION: ·

··· WINE/VARIETY: ·····································

··· DATE TASTED: ·····································

··· REGION: ·····································

··· VINTAGE: ·····································

··· APPEARANCE AND COLOR: ·····················

··· NOSE: ·····································

··· PALATE: ·····································

··· CONCLUSION: ·····································

Wine. The intellectual part of the meal.

—ALEXANDRE DUMAS

·· WINE/VARIETY: ···

·· DATE TASTED: ··

·· REGION: ···

·· VINTAGE: ··

·· APPEARANCE AND COLOR: ·································

·· NOSE: ···

·· PALATE: ···

·· CONCLUSION: ··

··· WINE/VARIETY: ·····································

··· DATE TASTED: ·····································

··· REGION: ·····································

··· VINTAGE: ·····································

···APPEARANCE AND COLOR: ·····················

··· NOSE: ·····································

···PALATE: ·····································

··· CONCLUSION: ·····································

pleasing pairings *

Write down various wine and food pairings
you've successfully served as well as new
pairing ideas you want to try.

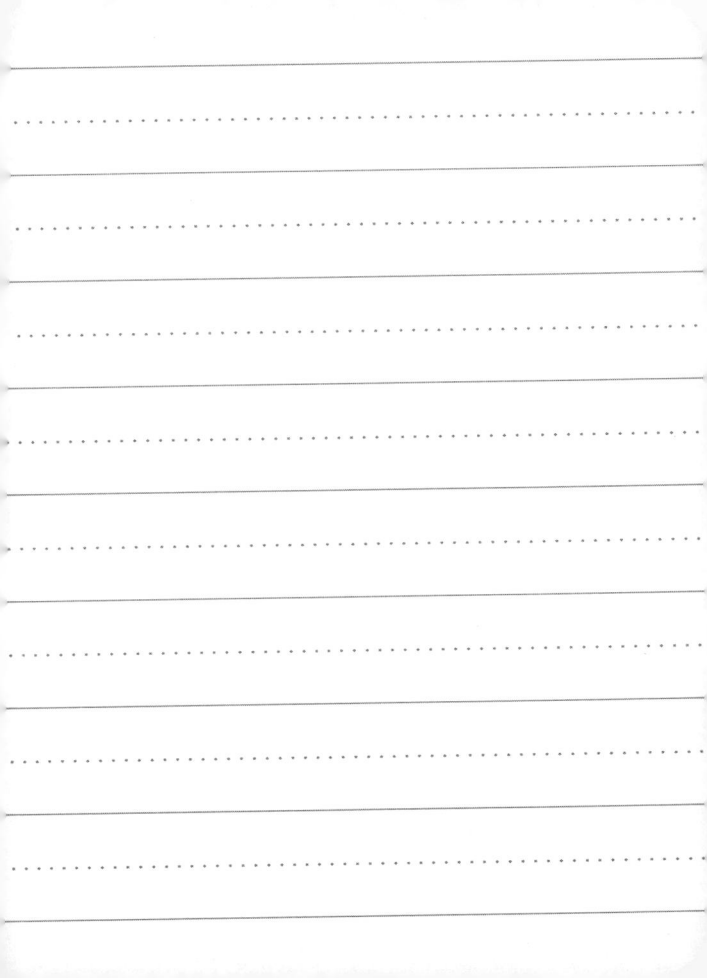

· · WINE/VARIETY: ···

· · DATE TASTED: ···

· · REGION: ···

· · VINTAGE: ···

· APPEARANCE AND COLOR: ···

· · NOSE: ···

· PALATE: ···

· CONCLUSION: ···

─────────────────────────── assorted wine ─

··· WINE/VARIETY: ···

··· DATE TASTED: ···

··· REGION: ···

··· VINTAGE: ··

··· APPEARANCE AND COLOR: ··

··· NOSE: ···

··· PALATE: ···

··· CONCLUSION: ···

··· WINE/VARIETY: ···

··· DATE TASTED: ···

··· REGION: ···

·· VINTAGE: ···

·· APPEARANCE AND COLOR: ·································

·· NOSE: ···

·· PALATE: ···

·· CONCLUSION: ···

··· WINE/VARIETY: ···

··· DATE TASTED: ···

··· REGION: ···

··· VINTAGE: ···

··· APPEARANCE AND COLOR: ·································

··· NOSE: ···

··· PALATE: ···

··· CONCLUSION: ···

··· WINE/VARIETY: ································

··· DATE TASTED: ································

··· REGION: ································

··· VINTAGE: ································

··· APPEARANCE AND COLOR: ························

··· NOSE: ································

·· PALATE: ································

·· CONCLUSION: ····························

· · · WINE/VARIETY: ·

· · · DATE TASTED: ·

· · · REGION: ·

· · · VINTAGE: ·

· · · APPEARANCE AND COLOR: ·

· · · NOSE: ·

· · · PALATE: ·

· · · CONCLUSION: ·

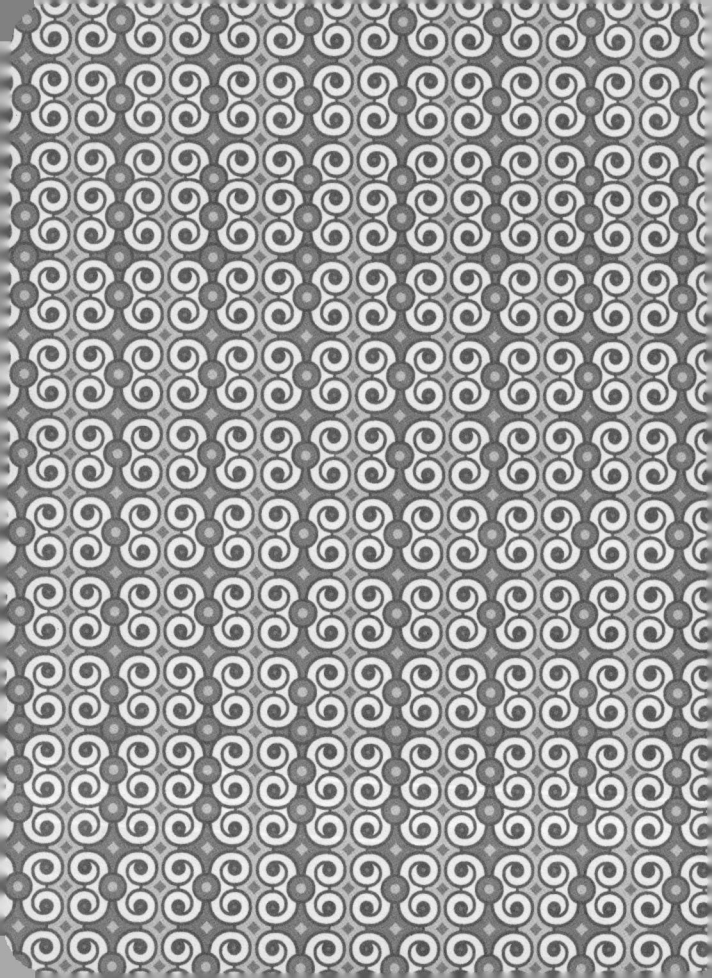